PRAISE FOR THE LEADER OF THE BAND

"Scott and his team helped our team at Great Western Bank grow from a $1 billion bank group to an $8 billion bank. His team was great at embedding themselves in our business and helping us put together an integrated plan of long term profitable growth. Scott was always working toward how to market both internally and externally to our constituencies. We both always focused on being honest and straightforward in all we did for our business. In the end, while we had great success together, the best thing I got out of the relationship with Scott was a good friend."

Jeff Erickson
Entrepreneur & Developer

"For well over a decade, I've worked with Scott and his co-workers at Lawrence & Schiller. From his work for state tourism, to highway safety, to my own political campaign, Scott and his team have been creative and diligent, with great attention to 'getting it right.' Scott leads by example, with personal attention to clients and employees alike. Scott has been a great leader at Lawrence & Schiller!"

Dennis Daugaard
South Dakota Governor

"One of the greatest movies of all time is *The Music Man*, where Robert Preston portrays an ambitious outsider, who comes into a sleepy, little town and stirs up excitement in their static world. In the end, *The Music Man* inspires a purpose and a sense of pride among the townsfolk. Scott Lawrence was Wakonda's Music Man . . . only with longer hair.

Mr. Lawrence transformed what was formerly a mere high school music curriculum into an entity all its own—The Wakonda High School Band. With new, stylish marching band uniforms, an updated repertoire of contemporary songs that were fun to perform, and marching routines that were beyond our small-town imaginations, Mr. Lawrence drove Wakonda's High School Band program into new directions, becoming a source of pride for the school and community.

For those of us involved, Wakonda's Band program (Marching Band, Concert Band, Pep-Band and Jazz Band) became our sense of purpose. Mr. Lawrence saw talent and potential in us that we didn't even recognize or cared to believe existed in ourselves. His encouragement inspired our dedication and led us to take ownership of our band program. Through that sense of unity, we developed a passion for pursuing excellence. Though our concert and contest performances were the end goals, practicing together and improving as an ensemble was our reward.

Those were truly some of the best memories from any time in my life. And, looking back, it's fascinating to see all of the important life and leadership lessons that were central to the whole experience. The transformation of Wakonda's High School Band program, from a typical music course in a small-town high school, to a remarkable and award-winning performing group, included many of the hallmarks of success: vision, ambition, coaching, dedication, hard work, improvising, and teamwork. And at the center of all of that was Mr. Lawrence—the Leader of the Band. But, most of all, we had fun . . . because Mr. Lawrence made it fun. And maybe that's the best part of those memories and perhaps the most important lesson to be learned."

Ryon Larson
Band Student

"I've had the pleasure of working side-by-side with Scott for three decades as he's led the band at Lawrence & Schiller. His boundless energy, ambitious goal setting, and genuine interest in every team member has inspired our shop to become a high-performance agency, 100% committed to winning and growing. L&S wouldn't be what it is today without Scott's vision and drive, and I owe much of my career success to the opportunities he's created for me.

Outside of my family, no one has made a bigger difference in my life than Scott Lawrence."

John Pohlman
Executive Vice President, Executive Creative Director,
Lawrence & Schiller

"I had the privilege of working with Scott at Lawrence & Schiller for nearly thirteen years. He has an infectious enthusiasm and a charisma that galvanizes his team around a common mission. As a leader, Scott taught me the importance of hiring the right people and giving them the authority and autonomy to thrive. If you hire better than yourself and get out of the way, good things happen."

Micah Aberson
Chief Global Brand Officer, Sanford Health

"I've been working with Scott Lawrence for over twenty-five years. He is a passionate, progressive leader who is focused on readying for whatever the future brings. He delivers for clients and team members, and is able to get people to produce their best work. Longevity in the agency business is rare, and Lawrence & Schiller's enduring success is a testament to Scott's leadership. *The Leader of the Band* provides details of Scott's successful leadership philosophy and practices."

Pat McAdaragh
President & CEO, Midco

THE LEADER

OF THE

BAND

THE LEADER OF THE BAND

**LEADERSHIP LESSONS FROM THE
KIDS WHO MADE ME A BETTER CEO**

SCOTT LAWRENCE

Cover Design: Les Cotton
Layout Design: Les Cotton and David Saldaña-Rico
Lead Writer: Angela Tewalt
Editor: Cameron Brooks
Publishing Manager: Brooke Brown

Throne Publishing Group
2329 N. Career Ave #241
Sioux Falls, SD 57107
ThronePG.com

DEDICATION

This book goes out to my lovely wife, Marlys, my children Elizabeth and Ralph, and the great employees and clients I have had the opportunity to work on great campaigns with. Also, I will never forget the students I had the opportunity to work with in my six years of Leading The Band. I thank all of you!

TABLE OF CONTENTS

FOREWORD

The agency business continues its rapid transformation. While omnichannel media consumption is making it more difficult to chase down audiences, those who adapt see technology as a new world of opportunity. While clients are demanding tangible business impact, those who adapt see the competitive advantage in more effectively correlating their work to outcomes. And, while client relationships continue their shift to project in nature, those who adapt see it as a means to systematically steal the business from their stagnant roster agency brethren.

Complicating the situation further is a new generation of talent with needs that are nothing like we've seen before—where quality of life and a deeper sense of meaning is fundamental. Believing in what they do and being motivated by their work is a basic requirement, no matter the role.

In contrast, early in my agency life, I remember believing it a privilege to be called on to take the lead on projects and work long hours into the night, if not for several weeks at a time. Part of moving up was to demonstrate a willingness to do whatever it takes to get the job done. Like a soldier being summoned to battle directly by the general, there was no doubt in my dedication. My motivation was to prove my mettle to a tough, tough boss who often ruled with a sense of do-it-or-I'll-find-someone-else-who-will. I was fortunate, after all, just to have this opportunity; to have this job.

Like the ancient ruins of a past civilization, long, relentless "work for the sake of work" hours are out. A more personalized, flexible and meaningful career is in. Moreover, why even stay in one job when life provides so many options to explore? In fact, recent research indicates turnover in the agency business to be more than 30% annually.

How is it possible to lead such a fickle new force when everyone has such personal needs? How is it possible to balance this with the pragmatic needs of a business ultimately driven by revenue growth?

And then, your senior team members. While dedicated, do they have the skills required for a radical new generation of marketing?

Getting the most out of talent has never been more challenging. And, we all know, getting the most out of talent has never been more critical for a growth-starved industry.

Scott Lawrence has some answers.

Over the past several decades, I've been fortunate to work at some great agencies like Wieden+Kennedy, TBWA, and Leo Burnett. Now at Mirren, I've worked intimately with several hundred CEOs and their teams on the method, motivation and accountability to drive new business and organic growth. However, as I reflect back, there is one CEO who stands out.

Working with Scott and his team, there is an energy that permeates the entire agency. There is something different. People are motivated. They are inspired. There's a chemistry. And, they are focused on mission critical growth—on collectively driving the agency forward.

More importantly, the way in which Scott interacts with his team is different. He has created deeply personal connections with his people—and between his people and their work. I've always believed that the foundation for effective leadership is to provide a vision for the organization that motivates; alignment of the team as they see each other within that vision; and then the operational support to execute.

Scott has some fascinating lessons to share. He really is the band leader in a time where we need a little harmony. I am so pleased to see him capture his insight in this book.

Take this book. Read it. Take advantage of his timeless leadership wisdom and apply it to your team."

Brent Hodgins
Mirren Business Development

INTRODUCTION

When I was a kid, my mom and dad were in the Columbia Record Club and regularly received new albums in the mail. All the time, we were putting new records on—always had the stereo going. The music never stopped, and I can still hear the record turning today. It's a beautiful sound, that music.

For a while, my dad was in the dance band. Every Saturday night, he'd have a gig. After the show, the guys would all come over and Mom would fix them breakfast. "I want a good egg, and I want it bad!" the drummer would say. I would sneak down to watch the guys yuck it up late at night. I grew up with that stuff. Music was everywhere in the home.

Mom and Dad were in the church choir. Dad was a great soloist. He would also play the bugle for taps at Memorial Day services, and they would both play piano in the home. My brother and I took piano lessons starting around second grade, and I picked up the trombone around fifth. Man, I loved music.

In high school, I discovered the bass guitar. Our band director was great and brought in this funky new instrument with a big Fender amp, and I was immediately drawn to it. Up until that point, all I had known was upright bass. I was a big Chicago fan and had heard bass in their music, but not until I saw THE bass guitar did I realize how much I loved bass. So I picked it up and started equating where the notes were on the neck with reading music and taught myself how to play. Just more music in my life. All the music, all the time.

By junior year, I got a band together. Sol, we called it, which is Swedish for sun, and we played with a foreign exchange student from Sweden. Oh, he was great, even friends with the guys from Abba before Abba was big. Anyway, we had synthesizers and smoke machines and pyrotechnics, and we had FUN. We performed at dances and bars and even got on stage at the World's Fair our senior year.

I tried to keep up the band in college. It was always morphing into something new. But I played football, loved sports just as much as music, and I remember one night seeing the marching band at a football game and thinking, God, I miss that. So I started jazz band and was in the practice room one day playing trombone, singing a few licks along with it, when there was a knock on the door. It was the choir director.

"ARE YOU A MUSIC MAJOR?" HE ASKED.

"NOT YET," I RESPONDED.

"HUH." HE WAS A STERN GUY. "WHAT DO YOU GOT ON MONDAYS, WEDNESDAYS, AND FRIDAYS AT THREE?" HE CONTINUED. I TOLD HIM INTRO TO BUSINESS, AND HE SAID, "NOT ANYMORE!"

WE GOT IN HIS CAR, AND HE DROVE ME STRAIGHT TO THE REGISTRAR'S OFFICE.

"HE'S DROPPING INTRO TO BUSINESS TO TAKE CHOIR WITH ME," HE COMMANDED. AND THAT WAS THAT. I NEVER TOOK ANOTHER BUSINESS COURSE AGAIN.

But I reveled in the music. I was in Madrigals, two jazz bands, orchestra concert choir, you name it. I may run a business today, and I love what I do, but I couldn't do it without the music. It keeps me ticking. Amid the work over the years, in my office and in my home, well, that music's playing, and music is everything.

I'm a fast guy. I'm ambitious and competitive and always wanting to win the game, but the music slows me. There's peace in the movement of a song, there's honesty within a melody, and it's amazing to realize how much I have learned just by having music in my life. I was a band director for my six years out of college, and to this day, I learned all my tips teaching music. If you pay close enough attention, you'll realize the lessons and wisdom and the insight you need to succeed in life are all right there in front of you, playing out amid the journey. Just listen, it's all there.

Music and leading the band taught me a lot, and now I want to share it with you. To my wife, my family, my band students, and all the folks at Lawrence & Schiller—thank you for the music.

FIRST JOB

CHAPTER ONE

COFFEE IN THE KITCHEN

was a twenty-one year-old band director when I had my first cup of coffee. My buddies at college would drink it to stay up all night and cram for finals, and I remember thinking then, *What's the big deal?* But in 1978, when I came to teach at my first job in South Dakota, I finally had my first cup, and that's when everything changed.

It always begins with a cup of coffee, doesn't it?

I graduated from the University of South Dakota in December of 1977. A few weeks later, I found myself wandering the halls at my new job, not knowing anyone, new to town, and anxious. It's easy to think you know what you're getting yourself into based off an interview or what you think you observe, but assumptions can be wrong, unfamiliarity can be daunting, and I needed to STEP UP.

My wife, Marlys, was also teaching at the same school. When I was offered a job, they offered her a job too, so that helped to ease the transition, but she would always go to the teacher's lounge. By my second week on the job, I was sitting over in the band room by myself. The shop teacher next door wasn't that fun to talk to, so I finally thought, *Well, I'm just going to venture out, and I'm going to go to the kitchen.*

There were two cooks. One was tall and slender and lived right in town near the school. The other was shorter and not as slender, and she lived on a farm about two miles outside of town. My wife and I would buy lamb burgers from her husband who raised sheep. Anyway, when I walked into the kitchen that first time, I just started talking to them.

"OH, YOU'RE THE NEW BAND DIRECTOR, RIGHT?" THEY ASKED.

"YEAH, I'M SCOTT."

"YEAH, WE KNEW THAT." OF COURSE THEY DID.

THEN, THEY ASKED IF I WOULD LIKE A CUP OF COFFEE.

"I'D LOVE A CUP OF COFFEE!" I REPLIED.

I had never tried it before, but what else was I supposed to do? They were drinking it, they offered it to me, and I wanted to be nice and oblige. So I did, and you know what? I kind of liked it! Before long, I was eating along with it homemade rusk with peanut butter, and I started learning a *whole lot of things* about the school and the community. Those ladies just knew everything about what was going on. Oh, they were telling me about who was doing what, which kids you wanted to get close to, which kids you wanted to look out for, how teachers would react to certain things, who you wanted to partner with, and who you wanted to avoid. You name it, we were talking about it!

Soon enough, that cup of coffee changed the trajectory of what my career was going to be in my first year of teaching. Every morning, I'd meet the cooks in the kitchen, and I'd help them pull things out of the freezer, help them get ready for fish sticks and peas or whatever lunch might be that day. And every time, I'd learn something new about the local gossip in town or whatever was going on in the school. I paid attention, and it was paying off.

I was so intrigued that I thought if coffee in the kitchen is working out so well, I should go to the coach's office and start doing the same thing with the folks there, too. So I did. I found out what was going on in their lives, learned about star athletes and aspirations they had for their teams, and soon enough, I was folding towels in the locker room during my free periods.

From there, I ventured to the teacher's lounge and developed the same rapport with the elementary school teachers. Now, high school teachers never had any contact with elementary, but I went down there anyway and would yuck it up through the haze of the smoke, and I would talk to them about the kids. I would especially buddy up with the fifth grade teachers, because I was going to be teaching those fifth graders in band soon, and I wanted to be ready for them.

It was about more than coffee. The coffee was good, I liked the buzz, but I was building relationships. And our conversations weren't just about the school or the small town, it was about them—their families, what they liked to do for fun. I wanted each person to understand that I cared about them as individuals as well as colleagues. I liked listening, and they appreciated being heard.

I got to know my students, too! They called me "Mr. L," and I spent a lot of time building a nice rapport with them as much as I could. There were some senior tough guys who weren't in the band, but I got to know them during a study hall I had with them, asking them about athletics. I enjoyed high school athletics a lot, so Marlys and I would go to all the tournaments and away games, and they knew we were big supporters. That mattered to them. I was building relationships, and it mattered.

COFFEE IN THE KITCHEN AT THE AGENCY

At Lawrence & Schiller, I spend a significant amount of time just walking around the agency, making it a practice to know everybody's name in the building. If I used to have eighty kids in the band and knew all their names, surely I can know and understand every person who is in the building at L&S. I also like to know what their kids' names are, what they like to do on the weekends, what high school they are from, what college they attended, and what they studied. I just get to know them a little bit, build a RELATIONSHIP with them.

I try to be helpful, too. Just like I was helping in the kitchen at my first job, I load the dishwasher at the office and clean out the fridge every couple weeks. Not only do I like a clean fridge, I'm not going to ask somebody to do something I wouldn't do myself. Doing this builds teamwork, and it builds a culture that isn't just about handing somebody a paycheck. It's a culture that CARES, and I think that helps in performance, because employees feel like there is some kind of vesting going on. That feels good. Everybody wants to feel a part of something, as they should.

Getting to know people starts with intentionally walking over to the kitchen and having a cup of coffee. I learned this affinity from those dear cooks years ago, and it's a part of my life to this day. Every morning when I get to work, the first thing I do is get a cup of coffee and move around the building. When you know your people, you run your business better. When you see your employees for *who they are*, you understand them better, you appreciate them more, and they feel invested in the business, too. Take the time to move around!

It wasn't easy starting out at my first job when I was barely older than my own students, but I took initiative to LEARN. You can go into a situation and let it control you, or you can go into a situation and do your best to help people understand that you are willing, committed, and that you care. If you want to plan for your future, get out and build relationships that will help you move that plan forward.

LEADERSHIP LESSON

Take the time to get to know people. Go out of your way to strike up conversations, ask questions and remain curious, because those relationships will benefit you and your business in the long run. Let people know you are interested in them, and they will be interested in you. March for them, and they will march for you.

CHAPTER TWO

THE WEDGE

When I was growing up in marching band, it was the same stuff all the time. There were no band competitions or events. You played your instrument, learned the same songs and maybe did a homecoming parade or nice little concert in the fall and spring. That's all we knew, that's what we did.

But just like the proliferation of tournaments and competitions in sports, the environment began to change, and band soon became a place where, if the kids were going to participate in all the competitions, they wanted to WIN. Not only did they want to have fun, they wanted to be a part of something that was a winner. So when I became a band director, I knew I had to build a program around whatever would satiate the kids' desire to WIN.

Everybody wants to win. We all know this feeling. But if you want it, you really have to *change* and adapt to whatever it takes to get there. Participation doesn't cut it. If you want to win, it's about hustle and effort, pomp and circumstance, and being a part of something BIG. And those kids wanted it.

Or maybe it was me. Maybe I wanted to win! But either way,

I began to study the people and the programs that were winning. What street formations were they running? What cadences were they playing? Who was arranging music? Who was writing shows? To figure all this out, I really had to form a band director "ilk." I was talking to different directors around the region, paying attention to everyone's shows, really trying to figure out what was *going on* in the industry. And I knew we had to change.

Up until that point, the traditional marching band formation was eight across and as far back as you could go in your ranks. Two step intervals in between, and just a big marching BLOCK. You'd put your brass up front so you could make a big impression coming down the street, percussion in the middle, woodwinds in the back then flags in front or back. That was the marching band formation, that's the WAY IT WAS. It's how we were taught, and it's how we did it.

Well then, these innovators started to do some things. They started to get these wacky ideas of maybe doing a different formation, and you started to see "The Wedge," a formation shaped like an arrowhead. First, you'd put your number one trumpet player right at the tip of the wedge so you could feature them or maybe they'd perform a solo if you so desired. Then, the drum majorette would be up front, flags would deploy along the wedge, percussion in the middle, woodwinds in a backward wedge, and tuba player at the very back tip so the whole band could hear the bottom—I'm a bass guy, remember. I love my tubas.

Now, when I told my kids we were going to do this new formation, you would've thought the world was going to end.

"WHAT! MR. L, ARE YOU CRAZY? WE CAN'T DO THAT!"

But we needed change. They were getting comfortable! We'd get out there, hit the streets to practice, they'd get in their formation, and it was like second nature. They weren't even trying. And what happens in your mind when you're comfortable? You don't concentrate! I knew these kids needed change.

So I drew it all out on the board, and they just stared with their mouths gaping. "Really, Mr. L?!" YES, REALLY. When we first tried it, man, they were stumbling. But you know what? *They loved it.* They got juiced. It was like instantaneous excitement, and once they figured it out, they couldn't wait to march somewhere. When we marched at Centerville's Homecoming, we deployed "The Wedge" for the first time, and, oh, the crowds loved it. Now, I got a few looks . . . *My, that's interesting* . . . but the kids were loving it, the change was good.

From there, we took on innovation by storm. We got new corps style uniforms, and when we marched, the judges loved it. We wanted to have a fresh look on the street, and "The Wedge" bumped our points, absolutely. Kids were having a blast, they thrived off the change, and we started winning!

ARE YOU THE BLOCK OR THE WEDGE IN THE AD INDUSTRY?

In the world of advertising, keeping up is practically impossible, but if you don't at least understand that change is critical, you will become trapped on Old Island, and you will become irrelevant. You will run out of water and food quickly, and you will die. Yes, it is that serious. You change, or you die.

If you are going to play the game, you have to play the game *to win,* and you have to understand what is going on in your industry. There are seminars and conferences to keep you abreast, and the best thing you can do is get out there, hear what is going on in the industry and build relationships with other people who are doing what you're doing in the business. Get out there, have coffee in the kitchen, try to keep up.

The ad agency is constantly under pressure. There is always change! But if you continue to push yourself to learn—IF YOU ARE HUNGRY—you will triumph. If you adapt, you will win.

Do not be intimidated by innovation. It is nothing new, people! It has been a part of our world forever; it is how we grow. The kids didn't want a new marching band formation, but when they accepted the challenge, they loved it and they WON. Innovation and change is about leadership accepting the fact that good is never good enough. You must always pursue greatness, knowing that you will never achieve it. For as soon as you think you are great, you will lose, and you will be back on Old Island. If you think you have the world by its tail—if you become too *comfortable*—you have lost the game, man, and who wants to lose?

You must always be moving and shaking. Do not get stagnant; comfort is a BAD THING. Now, I want people to *feel good* about who they are and the work they are producing, but I want them to feel *challenged* in that. The way it is done now is not going to be good enough forever, so we must grow, adapt, change, WIN.

I will admit, change is a delicate issue, because change is hard, and there are a lot of tedious steps in the process. But if you've had coffee in the kitchen and you've been building your leadership team, getting to know your people, you've conquered half the battle. When you are willing to change, you are capable of being the best. Go and BE THE BEST.

LEADERSHIP LESSON

If you want to grow, you must be willing to change. Change can be difficult, but it is also exhilarating and refreshing, and you need that positive energy to survive. If you are willing to change, you can WIN.

CHAPTER THREE

SENIORS ARE GRADUATING

By the spring of 1980, Marlys and I were having a lot of fun and some serious success. We were loving the teaching gigs. Our program had won a number of jazz band contests and marching contests. The community was really starting to buy into our efforts and everybody was getting into this deal.

We also had some great musicians. The kids had done well in solo contests, and we really had developed a nice group of senior leadership, including an outstanding trap drummer, trombone and trumpet player, as well as a base guitarist and keyboardist. We truly had a tremendous year and many seniors who were LEADERS.

As the year was finishing up, we started to get all these graduation invitations in the mail. One night, I got really choked up. I really loved these kids. I got really attached! They are just like employees, you know? I cared about them, they meant a lot to me, and knowing these kids were going to be done and that I was no longer going to see them in the band room really got to me. It was hard.

When I started my first teaching job in the spring semester of

'78, those kids were sophomores. They were just starting to find their groove in the band program, so I worked hard with them. We really had fun and built a program together. They were my bunch, they were my kids, and seeing these invites in the mail meant CHANGE.

So as I was going through the invitations, I said to Marlys, "What am I going to do? All my seniors are graduating!" She simply said, "You'll be just fine. You've got lots of sophomores and juniors. You'll *be fine*."

And she was right. Next fall, the seniors were gone, and guess what, those sophomores and juniors STEPPED UP to the plate. They had all grown up a year. They had been watching and listening and patiently WAITING for their turn to show what they could do. We continued to march on. The sophomores and juniors made me just as proud as the senior leaders before them. If anything, they in some ways took on their new role more effectively than the seniors before them. Those kids excelled. We didn't lose a step.

It's important to understand that you never *neglect*. Those original groups of seniors were key leaders for our band program, but that didn't mean I could discount the others. Conversely, I had to cultivate and DEVELOP all the young kids who I knew had the talent but weren't quite there yet. So instead of neglecting them, I had to *bring them along* and keep them ready for when those seniors graduated. I knew their time would come.

To build trust and confidence in these young kids, I gave weekly lessons. Every fifth, sixth, seventh, and eighth grader got a half hour a week with me, and it was a great recruiting tool. I would play along with whatever instrument they were playing, guide them along, but I was looking for talent, too, and paying attention to which kids wanted to WIN. Now the older kids could opt in for lessons if they wanted, and some did, but I made sure I had time for the young students so I could get to know them and really build the BIG PICTURE.

As for those sophomores and juniors coming in, I learned to give them the opportunity to be *comfortable* in the program while *challenging* them just as much as the senior leaders above them. I wanted them to feel valued and understood, and I wanted them to know I cared about them so that when they became seniors, they were READY, willing, and excited to take on their leadership role. I built a rapport with these kids, and it mattered.

I remember one spring, I walked into the band room, and there was this kid—not yet a part of the band program—just pounding on the drum set, playing really well.

"WHAT ARE YOU DOING?" I ASKED HIM.

"I WANT TO PLAY TRAP DRUM IN THE JAZZ BAND, SIR," HE SAID TO ME.

"I'VE BEEN WORKING ON IT AT HOME."

I could tell he had been, but he was such an unsuspecting kid! Always sneaking into the band room just to mess around, but we brought him in. He took over on the trap drums that season, and he didn't miss a beat. He was fantastic! But I spent time with him and encouraged him, because I saw the hunger. He had the music in him, he was READY, and he excelled.

I loved encouraging him. It was always important to me to inspire the kids, to provoke their talent so they were not only ready to be leaders when their time came, but so they *enjoyed* the music. When I wasn't giving a lesson, I always used to put on jazz tapes in the background, Maynard Ferguson or Buddy Rich, just so the kids could hear it and kind of *emulate*, you know? If we weren't playing music, we had it on all the time, just like I did at home growing up, and it was another way to build leadership in the band program. Whether they were a fifth grader or a senior about to fly, every student played a role in the band.

SAY GOODBYE TO YOUR SENIORS WELL

If you are doing your job correctly as a CEO today, you are constantly *cultivating* talent, and you do it knowing fully well those "seniors" will someday leave you. But when that time comes, you wish them the best, you say, "Go get 'em, tiger, this is what you've worked for, YOU GOT THIS," and send them off. Away they go.

I have had the opportunity in my career to train CEOs, managers, and business owners who all started with me. I would find them in college, mentor, and spend time with them, then watch them walk out my door because they were ready to fly. They continue to soar today.

It is not easy saying goodbye to talent. There's nervousness around that, but you must do so with the expectation that there are others still in the building READY for their shot. They've been waiting in the wings, but when it's their turn to go on stage, LOOK OUT, they will impress you. Those "sophomores" and "juniors" always do.

But if you want them to rise to the occasion, you've got to train, encourage, and spend time with them just as much as you do your senior leaders. EVERYONE MATTERS. As a CEO, it is incumbent upon you to be sure you are recruiting and hiring and doing your very best to find good talent. *Then*, once you've got them, it is incumbent upon you to get to know them, have a little coffee in the kitchen and build relationships so they feel a part of something.

For some employees, it takes longer to acclimate than others, but give everyone the space they need, and guide them along the way. This is building the BIG PICTURE—recruiting and nurturing those who will be LEADERS for you every step of the way. You've got this.

LEADERSHIP LESSON

Build your team. Build your band. Encourage young talent while supporting senior leaders, and then when those seniors leave you, trust that your recruitment efforts will pay off, because the young bucks will step up to the plate and prevail.

CHAPTER FOUR

GRASS IS NOT ALWAYS GREENER

N ow even though we had good success, obviously there was competition. Every school does. Competition is a great thing, and I believe that wanting to win is a big part of being successful. So of course, in the four years at my first teaching job, there was always that ONE program we couldn't beat. Oh, they always looked good, had some great musicians, and were fun to watch.

One February evening, I got a call at home, and it was from THEM. It was the superintendent of our biggest competitor, the one to beat, and they were calling ME.

"HEY, SCOTT, I WAS WONDERING IF WE COULD TALK WITH YOU ABOUT TAKING OVER OUR BAND PROGRAM," HE SAID SO COOLLY.

AT FIRST, I WAS DISMISSIVE. "OH, I DON'T KNOW, I'M PRETTY HAPPY HERE," I REPLIED. BUT HE KEPT ON.

"WELL, LET'S JUST TAKE A LOOK, OKAY?" HE INVITED MY WIFE AND I OVER FOR A BAND CONCERT, AND HE MADE AN OFFER.

Oh, gosh, we hemmed and hawed. For a month and a half, we went back and forth trying to make a decision. It was agony thinking about it for that long! At the time, we really couldn't figure out why it was so alluring to us other than the fact that it was THE program we couldn't beat, you know? I was always watching them, they were so disciplined, and I remember thinking to myself, *this could be cool.*

The more I was intrigued, the more they kept calling and pushing. To be honest, I kept trying to put this thing on the back burner. We were happy! But then one night, they called and offered to double my salary. Come on. That got our attention, so we got pretty serious, and we decided we were going to go for it. It would involve a move, a change of schools, but Marlys and I agreed. *We were going to do this.*

Now we had built a great program over the past four years. We had a lot of heart and soul in that little town, and that program was OURS. Not only that, we had some great friends and built meaningful relationships. It was hard to let that go. When we first announced we were making the move, it was just, "WHAT! That's our enemy!" Then, oh, gosh, the kids started chiming in, "Mr. L! You can't do this to us! Come on, Mr. L!" The band was crushed. They didn't get it. Even the *parents* went on, taking us out to dinner, trying to convince us to change our minds. We even had a farmer offer us two acres of land on the bluff to build a house on and stay. *It was that serious.*

The superintendent was understanding, but disappointed. He asked why, and I was honest. It was about opportunity, more money! But making that announcement in the spring and then having to finish out the school year was miserable. We were kind, went out with everybody, made the best of it, but in the back of my mind I thought, *just let this be over.* We endeavored to say goodbye well, and even though some people looked at us as traitors, so many others wished us well, and to this day it's those people we remember most.

Summer of '82, we moved to our new school, new band program, new town. We were like strangers in a strange land. We had officially left our small town utopia behind to build a brand new program, and I'll tell you what, there was REGRET.

Here's the thing. I didn't trust my gut. At my first job, I had a brand new band room, nice facility, a school board that would buy us anything we needed, and a community that supported us fully. They loved us. Then when Marlys and I went to check out this new program, they were a darn good band, but their band room was shoved into the basement, and their facilities were not on par with the facilities we had in small town utopia. Moreover, it didn't feel as WARM and there was a lot of *expectation* in this new program that wasn't placed upon me before. The warning signs were there. It was obvious! *But we ignored the signs.* This was the WINNER, and all I saw was the winner—this shiny object in front of me I thought I HAD to have. But, sometimes, something you THINK is better isn't always everything you thought it would be. Money isn't everything, and the grass is NOT always greener; hardly ever is.

It just wasn't the same. We were comfortable where we were, we were having FUN. It sure didn't seem as much fun when I was trying to convince myself otherwise, but we were happy, and there were many days that we wished we were back on our little acreage, enjoying the life. Many days.

But I said I wanted this, so I got into it. Before the school year began, I started going over to the school, seeing who I could talk to, having coffee in the kitchen again, and it felt nice. I met the math teacher, we struck up a friendship, things really started rolling along. But in the back of my mind I thought, *What am I going to do here?*

It was different and I was tentative. I didn't approach the program with as much confidence or fidelity as I should have. *Did I do the right thing?* Over and over this was in my mind, and that would drag into my performance as I started out at this new gig. It was a tough go and, man, I struggled.

If I could turn back the hands of time and understand what we were leaving versus what we were going into, my decision might have been different. I did grow to love the kids and the community just the same, but it took a while, and I can see so clearly now that those four years at our first job were probably four of the best years we ever spent in our young married life. We left a really good thing. Good people, a good life.

ASSESS OPPORTUNITY BEFORE YOU SAY YES

Leaving that first job was an emotional time, but it was a good lesson. The grass really did look greener—it was double the money—but it was not the same. When you are faced with life-changing decisions—and you WILL be at some point in your career—you've got to trust yourself. If you see the red flags, assess them fully, understand the implications, then take your TIME. Do you really need the bright and shiny object in front of you, or do you just *want* it? Is vanity making the decision for you, or are you really doing what is best for yourself, your family, your career?

I spent two years at the new teaching gig, and they really were a great program. I enjoyed that time in my life and really grew to love the program, but I went there because I was attracted to the WINNER and attracted to the money. But when I got there, I had to start over and build a NEW band to make it my own and build from something that was already well in place. That was tough, like moving into somebody else's house!

When you take on something new, you cannot assume leadership right away and expect to be successful. *Leadership is gained, not earned,* and it took me a long while to establish leadership working for the competition.

As a CEO, you must be patient in building a rapport with your team, and you must trust the decisions you make every step of the way. If you've got employees who see the greener pastures like I did, say goodbye well, wish them the best, and trust your gut.

If a buyout opportunity approaches you, fully assess your options, and KNOW what you are getting yourself into. A buyout is about money, like everything else, so understand the toll there, and if it doesn't FEEL right, it probably isn't. Be a wise and careful leader, and take care of yourself. Every decision matters.

LEADERSHIP LESSON

If you're having a tough time making a big decision, you're not listening to your gut. The answer is always within you. Follow your heart in these things, pay attention to the signs, and do the right thing. Always do the right thing, and you will be successful.

PART TWO

NEW JOB

CHAPTER FIVE

WE LOST

T his new school was a well-oiled machine. They were practiced, they knew a lot of things, and they had their own groove, which meant it took me a while longer to get close with the kids. Everything took a bit of time for me, actually, but we put together our first marching show for our first fall competition, and we won. That was good.

But then we had our second competition. We got up at five in the morning, got to school, loaded percussion onto the bus, and the two ladies who always drove bus for us were all riled up with high expectations. "Oh, you better be WINNING today!" To be honest, I had trepidation in my stomach. I didn't feel good about things, the way I was relating to the kids. I was relating to them well in the system, but the kids in the band are like your employees in the office, you know? At the end of the day, THEY are the ones blowing the horns, the ones getting stuff done, and I just did not feel GOOD about the way things were going.

My gut was right, because, lo and behold, we got second place at the competition. And we got second place *to the program I had just left*. The program we could never beat when I was there finally lost, and I was on the other side of it all. And of course, I knew all the kids who had just won—I had just left them!—and they were giving me a hard time. "Hey, Mr. L, we just beat you!" Just a miserable ride home. Miserable Sunday. It was one of the hardest things. I had a pit in my stomach all weekend, just doubting myself and feeling miserable.

That Monday morning, we got to the band room and first thing I said was, "We gotta talk." And I laid it ALL out there for the kids. I told them everything I was feeling. I was honest! I said to them, "YES, we lost. *I'm sorry.*" But I assured them that I was NOT the same as their previous director. I told them change was coming. "I am going to do everything in my power to WORK WITH YOU to do the things we need to do to WIN." And they loved it. They responded! It was like I saw them for the first time. We saw each other. "You got it, Mr. L! Let's do this!" That felt good.

Losing to our rival was a turning point. It was a huge turning point, because things were not going WELL. I didn't like going to school! I was regretting my decision to move! I didn't have the connection and the discipline and the fearlessness to be the LEADER they needed me to be. I needed that loss to step up to the plate and finally assume position. IT WAS TIME to take control. Once I did, they responded, and everything changed.

We had this big kid—six feet four, good looking kid, dating the drum majorette, all-state basketball player and all that—and after I gave my big speech that Monday morning, he approached me.

"HEY, MR. L," HE SAID. "WE'LL GET 'ER DONE."

He came up to ME, approached ME and gave me the conviction

I needed to march on. And, BOOM, things just started rolling. Everything changed. Suddenly, there were smiles, energy, interaction, suggestions, ideas.

"WE'LL GET 'EM NEXT TIME, MR. L!"

And we did. Oh, we did. We triumphed that year.

All of a sudden, it was fun again. Before, I was all shook up because it was NEW. I was treading water . . . *Ohhh, I don't know how this is going to go, I don't know if I can do this* . . . Do you know what happens when you dance around things, and you don't get after it? You get half-assed results! You got to go for it! And I didn't. When I first got there, I was nervous. I was scared. I wasn't BEING ME, I wasn't pushing them hard enough and I was not assuming the CONTROL I had at my last job. I wasn't sure of myself, I was letting THEM be in charge, and that's not what they needed!

Everybody wants to know where the corral is. Kids need to know where the corral is, and if you haven't told them, they are going to push you until they find it. They need authority, and when I arrived weak and anxious, I didn't establish the corral. I was too CAREFUL not to change things, but, by golly, we started changing things and it made all the difference. We started WINNING, and we had a great year.

ESTABLISH AUTHORITY IN THE WORKPLACE

When you are in any leadership position in any facet of your life, you need to know that it is okay to lose. It is okay to stand in front of somebody and say, "I did not do as good of a job as I could have done with you. I screwed up, and you know what? I'm going to get better. I'm going to work on it, and we are going to work on this thing together." Now, how *you* do it might be DIFFERENT than somebody else, but you have got to be SURE that you will get your team to where they need to be. Those new kids needed me to be sure, and I failed them at first. But as soon as I admitted I was wrong—to both myself and to the band—we began to win.

If you make a mistake, one of the coolest things ever is to just admit that you were wrong and apologize. People appreciate honesty, humility, integrity. Do not be afraid to establish authority, and do not be afraid to screw up in that position. A great leader is not perfect! A great leader is human and humble, and you can be, too.

I cannot tell you how many times I've stood in front of the folks at L&S to say, "Hey, I wanted to do things this way, but I was wrong, and I'm sorry." Then we move forward. When I admitted to the band that I was unsure and then we lost, I established authority right then and there. "This was my fault, but we are going to fix it, and it starts with me." Buck stops here, baby! All right? Do you see what I'm saying? You must have conviction in your control, you cannot be passive about this. Passivity will make your employees and your clients aggressive, and you deserve better than that.

When we land a big client at L&S, do you think we're passive about it? Do you think we walk into the big meetings and say, "Well, you tell us how you want us to work with you, we'll do whatever you want." NO! We establish authority immediately. "Here is how we work with people; here is how this will go." Clients deserve that authority because there is clarity and comfort in it. There is a WAY we do things at L&S, we are very open and honest about it, and clients appreciate that. They will *ap-*

preciate you when you stand your ground and have conviction in your work.

TRUST your capabilities. You are there for a reason! Never betray yourself. You are a hell of a leader, so go for it. Trust yourself and WIN.

LEADERSHIP LESSON

In client relationships and with your team, assume responsibility, and have faith in your leadership. Trust your worth. Do not waste time being wishy-washy about this! Go forth with gusto, admit when you are wrong, move forward, and dominate. Go and LEAD.

CHAPTER SIX

NINETY-EIGHT DEGREES IN THE SHADE

W hat a crazy year this was. Marlys and I moved to our new job in the fall of '82, and by the spring of '83, we had some big news.

We got a letter in the mail from the National Independence Day Parade in Washington, D.C. asking us to audition for it. We needed to submit video and a record of our marching performances, so we did, and by that March, we got a letter back saying that we had been accepted. We were going to march down Constitution Avenue in the 1983 National Independence Day Parade on behalf of South Dakota. A *frenzy* of preparation began.

OH, we were jazzed. So excited. We started fundraising, looking at new uniforms, updating percussion lines, new flags, figuring out the show. Instead of playing our typical stuff on the street, I did an arrangement of patriotic tunes—some Sousa, "Stars and Stripes Forever"—it was the Fourth of July parade in our nation's capital! We were going patriotic, and the whole TOWN got into this. We would even head over to nearby communities to play concerts for them, and they would rally around us, too.

By May, we were practicing five nights a week. Police would

shut down Main Street so we could march downtown, and people would come out of their houses to hoot and holler. It was truly Americana at its finest, and it was absolutely great.

On July 2, we hopped on our tour bus and began our journey to D.C. We first drove to Springfield, Illinois, then arrived in Philadelphia late morning on July 3 for our first parade, right along the historic Liberty Bell. It was so exciting. Most of these kids hadn't even made a long-distance phone call before, let alone make it all the way to Philadelphia and D.C.!

We were feeling great, but it was HOT. We had been on our air-conditioned charter bus doing just fine, but as soon as the kids got off the bus in Philly, they were tired, and it was sweltering. It was so hot, the kids' shoes were sticking to the asphalt of the parking lot. I remember before we left, my wife came into rehearsal one night reminding the kids to pack antiperspirant deodorant to reduce the sweat rings, and, by golly, we needed it! We lost four kids during that parade route because they had to be taken to aid stations. It was just so hot – those poor kids.

We finished the parade there by late afternoon. Everyone got on the bus tired, sweaty, grumpy, uniforms all a mess, just in fits. The good news was we had finished that parade, the bad news was we had to be lined up on Constitution Avenue at 5 a.m. the next morning in D.C. We fought traffic, but didn't get to the hotel until 11:30 that night. Kids stumbled off the bus and into their rooms, and no sooner were they back on the bus, still grumpy and tired, only a few hours later.

And, it was still HOT. Even early in the morning, it was stiflingly humid, and conditions were perfect for meltdowns and half-assed performances. But you know what I thought? NOT TODAY. Marlys and I looked at each other and said, "Okay, we only have one option here, and that's to rock and roll."

So I went around to each section and started rousing the troops. "All right, let's line up! Let's start warming up! Keep your uniform top off, we're going to hammer this deal, folks, it's going to be good, it's going to be good." And, doggonit, their attitude was great. However I was reacting to things was how THEY were reacting to things; they needed me to be positive. In reality, I was worried about the weather, worried about kids dropping out, and this was a BIG DEAL marching down Constitution Avenue, but I could not let them see me sweat. So I kept passing around the waters and rallying the troops.

The parade started at 10 a.m., and right as we began the route, the clouds rolled in, and a little thunderstorm and a little rain broke through and cooled it down a good twenty degrees. Unbelievable, just perfect. We turned onto Constitution Avenue, and the kids just hammered it. They were so charged! I'll never forget it! I can still see and hear it so clearly in my mind. A little rain coming down, all these buildings around us and massive crowds just hollering and celebrating at the National Independence Day Parade in Washington, D.C. And our kids were right there, in the middle of it all, knocking it out of the park.

I was so proud of them. We had prepared and pushed ourselves, and they triumphed more than ever. They faced adversity and pressure to succeed, but they prevailed with enthusiasm, and I was in awe of their perseverance. That morning, it was ninety-eight degrees in the shade, but I fell in love with those kids. I was truly proud.

After the parade, we were euphoric. We got to listen to Neil Diamond perform on the National Mall with fireworks that night. The next day, a woman with the parade committee came to the hotel with a big trophy for us.

"Congratulations," she said. "You won the National Independence Day Parade." We did it. Indeed, after a long, hard year, we had absolutely WON.

HOW WILL YOU RISE TO THE OCCASION?

You will face adversity in business. You will face tough situations and losses. Over and over again. There will be setbacks, "hot days," and challenges every which way. So what are you going to do about it? How are you going to RESPOND to the adversity? Do you want your employees to see you kicking chairs and cussing about it and making a big fuss? Do you want your team to see you sweat? Come on. You want them to see you confident, with an answer and motivated to lead. If you lead in confidence, they will follow.

People are tougher than we give them credit for. So when you are in a leadership position, be tough, show your team the way and do not discount their own grit. People want to be challenged! My kids in D.C. were READY to take on the challenge. Bring on that heat! Bring on that rain! They were tested, *I was tested*, but we were dancing in the rain.

When you work hard, when you BELIEVE in your leadership skills and trust yourself, it all pays off. That trophy still stands today, proof of what a TOUGH year of hard work can do.

And teach along the way. As you prepare and practice and hone your skills to become a better leader, direct your people through it. We're all learning together. Life is about teaching, so embrace the opportunity, tell your team what you have gained, learn along with them, and ENJOY the win.

LEADERSHIP LESSON

Be ready to lead and be resilient in the face of hardship. There will be difficult times, but bring 'em on so you can use them as opportunities to show your team what you are made of. You are tougher than you know. Prove it.

CHAPTER SEVEN

THE EIGHTY–EIGHT AND THE TWO

W hen we started rehearsing that spring for the National Independence Day parade, I had some tough kids in the crowd. I remember we were all excited for this great opportunity, started marching, started playing the music, getting all pumped up, and I had some *eye rolls* from a couple percussion players. Oh, here we go.

It was just two kids. I had ninety kids in the band, and it was just two kids, yet I kept focusing on THEM every time we were trying to do this thing. Every day, we'd go out to march, and it did NOT seem like they were into it. It concerned me. Together, it had really been a growing year for us all; I was finally building credibility, finally getting along with the kids, and I wanted everybody in the fold. I wanted all the kids BUYING INTO what we were doing here. So I started doting on the two. "What's the matter here? You're not buying in, everything okay?" And this went on for weeks!

Finally, one night, Marlys and I were home eating supper, and she could sense something was up. So I told her that even though I really liked where we were going for this Fourth of July show, I had a couple kids who just weren't buying into it.

"Well, what about everybody else?" she asked. I told her they were loving it.

Then, she looked at me and said quite matter-of-factly, "Then why are you worrying about the two? You should be worrying about the eighty-eight! The two will take care of themselves." And she went on with her dinner, problem solved, just like that.

And what a GOOD POINT. I had been worrying about those two and giving them WAY too much of my attention for way too long, and for what? That wasn't doing me any good, only riling them up even more! She was absolutely right, and I tell you what, over the years, my most difficult problems have been solved by my wife. There is power in the partnership, a different perspective, and she has brilliant insight. Of course, her advice was spot on.

The next day, I went back to work with the band, stopped worrying about the wily two, really focused on polishing and getting better and getting this going, and a funny thing happened: the two became ZERO. The eighty-eight became the ninety. I had my band back, baby.

FOCUS ON THE GOOD

If you are convicted about the things you are trying to do for your business and continue to work for excellence no matter what, things will fall into place as they should. The worst that could happen? Somebody quits. And if they quit, I guess they didn't like the pressure or the challenge or they weren't a good fit in the first place. I quit doting on the two and really spent time working with the eighty-eight, right? And that's where I should have been all along. That is where you belong, too.

Work on your leadership team. Focus on your strengths, not on your weaknesses. Go for it and PUSH.

In business, we talk a lot about win and growth. When I present these things in meetings, I always get so charged up celebrating our growth, our initiative, giving them the real ra-ra speech. But I focus specifically on the fact that we are on a ride from good to great, and that we will never get to our destination if I have to focus on anything or anyone trying to slow us down. It'll be a fun ride, I tell them, but if you don't like looking ahead, then maybe this isn't the right place for you. I CHALLENGE them a little bit, and they love that! Of course, there's always a couple in the back not giving me the time of day, but I don't worry about them! I have learned you've got to worry about the eighty-eight.

You have a vision and a mission for what you want to achieve. Do not be dissuaded by the few who aren't ready for your greatness. Move on! It is your JOB to live up to what Spock said to Captain Kirk as he was dying in the engine room: "The needs of the many outweigh the needs of the few" (*Star Trek II: The Wrath of Khan, 1982*).

If you cater to everyone, you will cater to no one. Now, when it comes to my employees' well-being and their lifestyles and their families, I cater to everyone. I care deeply about my employees; I want them to be well. That is absolute. But when it comes to *understanding* the direction the company is going, I do not cater to each of them. They need to KEEP UP for themselves.

Years ago, we transitioned to self-directed teams at the agency, and that required some education components and a personal growth plan. It was a big shift. In business, there is always

CHANGE, but some of your employees might not like change. They might think they are already good enough, and if they do, that is their prerogative. LEAVE THEM BE. They might even push you, begging for your attention—for your doting, right? But amid any shift or attempt to GROW, let an employee decide for themselves if they are ready to fall in line and keep up with you. Meanwhile, focus on the good. See the strengths within your company, embrace the majority—the leaders forging *ahead*—you'll get your band all buying in eventually.

LEADERSHIP LESSON

Do not be paranoid. There is always good in business. Focus on your strengths, not on your weaknesses. Develop your strength, encourage your leadership team, and remain steadfast on your mission no matter who or what tries to derail you. Be the leader. March on.

CHAPTER EIGHT

WHAT'S THE TROPHY FOR?

have always wanted to win. I'm competitive and ambitious and on fire like that, and I believe if you ever lose that zeal-ousness to excel, you are on your way to extinction. So I'm constantly moving and shaking, and when I started teaching and directing band, it felt so good to share that desire to win with the kids. At both schools, I quickly instilled this culture of wanting to win, and they all loved it. They loved feeling a part of something. It's one of the best things about teaching; watching a student feel proud of his or her accomplishments.

I remember in my first teaching year, taking the kids to their first-ever marching band competition. Of course, we partici-pated in the ol' BLOCK formation, played a little *Roman Open-er*, got our flags up to speed. Did we win? No, not even close, but the kids got the TASTE. They saw who did win, and they were like, "Mr. L, WOW, look at their uniforms! Look how sharp they are!" They went on and on. "Yeah, you like that, kids? SO DO I, so let's start winning." And we did.

I just kept taking them to contests, exposing them to a winning environment and giving them the taste of playing the game to WIN, not just participate. We were better than participants! It didn't take long for their hunger to dominate; they were ready to get after it.

But in the beginning, I was missing a big part of the win. When we first started winning parades, we'd take home our trophies and our plaques, and we'd place them humbly on a shelf. We were proud and excited. I'd tell them, "Great job!" But then we'd get back to work on Monday. No rest! Let's get after it, right? We didn't make a big deal of it, and we moved on.

But then, I took the kids to the Augustana Jazz Festival. It was THE jazz festival to compete at, and we blew away our class. That night, we even got to play for a full audience at the Orpheum Theater in Sioux Falls. All their folks came to town to watch the kids perform on the big stage, and we took home a really nice trophy to add to that humble little shelf.

But that next morning, the basketball coach came by.

"I HEARD YOU GUYS DID OKAY YESTERDAY, HUH?" I SHOOK MY HEAD YES.

"WELL, IS THAT THE TROPHY OVER THERE?" HE CONTINUED. I SHOOK MY HEAD AGAIN.

THEN HE PERKED UP. "YOU SHOULD CELEBRATE THAT A LITTLE BIT!"

"WHAT DO YOU MEAN?" I ASKED.

"OH, IF WE WIN A TOURNAMENT SOMEWHERE, WE CELEBRATE THAT A LITTLE BIT. WE TALK ABOUT IT!"

And, you know what, I liked what he had to say. So I went over to the superintendent's office, told him we won a pretty big jazz festival last night and asked if we could get the kids out of school early, send them to the auditorium and play our concert for them.

"GREAT IDEA!" HE SAID. SO WE CELEBRATED.

The kids were so charged up. They LOVED that they got to perform in front of their peers, celebrate the trophy and ENJOY their hard work, and the whole school loved it, too. They went nuts! In that moment, there was no expectation, just joy and pride. As their leader, I had allowed it to become somewhat of an expectation to win. *We win, that's what we do. We put it on the shelf, onto the next one.* And that's good and well, but the kids really appreciated the unexpected opportunity to show their peers what they had been working on, and that meant a lot to them. It meant a lot to me, too. I still see those big smiles.

HONOR THE WORK

It's about more than celebrating the victories. It's about honoring the work. And not for long! Do not overemphasize being the best or number one; simply take a moment to honor the great work that was put in, then get back to work KNOWING you are capable of winning again. Remember, if you become too entitled in your successes, you begin to LOSE. Winners give thanks for the joy, embrace the good feelings and go back to honing their strengths until the next win comes around. If you win well, it always does.

Foster an environment of winning in your company. What is life if you're not winning? Life is always about feeling good and excelling! Just like I exposed my band kids to what it looked like to win, energize your employees and instill in them the courage and the MOXIE to succeed. Is it in your moxie to win? It better be or you are in the wrong business, my friend. Look to the wins. Desire to BE the winner, and you will be.

In an ad agency, winning comes in many different ways, but new business is the lifeblood. If you do not have an aggressive new business program, if you are not pitching and competing, your company will not win. If you are waiting for the business to come to you, you are entitled, and you are not winning. Go out, pitch, compete, and give your team the opportunity to taste it. They will become more aggressive and hard-working, which will only help you land better clients and more opportunities.

When I first got into the agency business, I noticed the same "humble trophy shelf" I had in my band days. We'd pick up new business, move on. That was the expectation, to just keep going. But then I asked my employees to do just a bit more. Whenever a team had a winning pitch, I asked them to give the presentation to our entire organization, in front of their peers. If it was good enough to WIN, it's good enough for other people in the building to watch and see what they might learn from it. They loved it.

Your peer group is the toughest group you'll ever pitch to, because you're always the most nervous in front of your people. It's a tough crowd, but it allows them to celebrate a little bit, show their peers all the hard work they've been doing, then we pop a little champagne in the production room and move on.

Leadership is about heading *toward* a destination, and the destination in the agency business is a happy client and a great culture for employees so you can ultimately grow business. We want success; success is winning, and celebration of the win *acknowledges the effort*. It's proof that passion exists within your company, the employees appreciate the work, and they want to keep your business running and successful. And THAT is something to celebrate.

LEADERSHIP LESSON

Praise the effort. Take a moment to see the trophy, celebrate how that feels in your arms, and give thanks for a job well done. We thrive when we become aware of our strengths. Don't rest in that glory, just acknowledge it, but honor the work, and go on to win. Again and again.

CONCLUSION

L eadership isn't easy. There will always be tough decisions, adversity, long days, CHANGE. But if you build relationships, trust and prove your worth, keep up, and focus on the good, you will win. Step away from the hustle, embrace the peace in the music every once in a while, and you will soar.

Before you get back to business, my final leadership lesson to you is this: Don't forget where it came from. I have been so richly blessed in this beautiful, musical life. And once I figured out that I am only the caretaker—that the music is not my song—everything became so much easier to manage. Mistakes were tolerable, decisions were easier to accept, because I had someone to lean on. You do, too, and you also are *capable* of winning this thing. You are worthy of the glory that is ahead of you. You've got this. GO. It's time to win.

ABOUT THE AUTHOR

For the last thirty-four years, Scott Lawrence has been working in the advertising industry with his company, Lawrence & Schiller. Scott started as an account executive, moved on to VP of Sales, became President, and eventually purchased the majority of the stock and became CEO. But, prior to all of this, Scott spent six years as a band director, and wow, what an education in leadership! This book is a fun journey through his days of teaching, and how it applies to a rapidly-changing industry. Scott has always had a love of music, and Lawrence & Schiller is his band. Scott lives in Sioux Falls, SD with his wife, Marlys, and their two children, Elizabeth and Ralph, who also live and work in Sioux Falls.

ABOUT LAWRENCE & SCHILLER

LAWRENCE & SCHILLER

Lawrence & Schiller was founded in 1976 in Sioux Falls, SD. Today L&S employs eighty people and does close to $40 million in gross billing with a diverse base of clients, mostly with a Midwestern footprint. The company believes strongly in change, outthinking and outdoing, and is very proud of its "family" culture.

Most agencies talk the talk. L&S walks the walk. Every day they strive to outthink and outdo, creating advertising and marketing strategies that are a little unexpected and a lot effective.

They are constantly adapting to embrace new innovations and trends in marketing. But one thing will never change: their dedication to helping clients tell their story in a way that's insightful, meaningful, and effective. From branding and design to media strategy, consumer research and digital marketing, Lawrence & Schiller goes all out to see your brand succeed.

www.ingramcontent.com/pod-product-compliance
Lightning Source LLC
Chambersburg PA
CBHW050512210326

41521CB00011B/2429